V10
BOOK OF
LIVED

Penny Authors

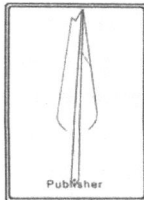

Publisher

MA PUBLISHER

Penny Authors

Produced by MAPublisher for Penny Authors
Email: Pennyauthors@yahoo.co.uk
www.pennyauthors.org.uk

Published by MA Publishing (Penzance)
Email: mapublisher@yahoo.com
www.mapublisher.org.uk

Released on August 2024

Printed in the region the books have been published: Australia | Canada | Europe | UK | USA

ISBN-13: 9781915958167

Cover designed by Mayar Akash
Typeset in Times Roman

Paper printed on is FSC Certified, lead free, acid free, buffered paper made from wood-based pulp. Our paper meets the ISO 9706 standard for permanent paper. As such, paper will last several hundred years when stored.

CONTENT

"I really want to thank you for all of your encouragement and kindness about my poetry, without which I am sure I wouldn't have had the confidence to keep writing."

Chloe Hall
Tavistock, UK

Introduction

Welcome to the 10th accomplishment of the Penny Authors' Anthology. The previous anthologies have laid and built a strong pathway for grass roots writers to take their maiden step to get their work championed in the national and global theatre of the written words.

The experiences that are captured in the anthology are colourful and the times that they've happened give it the flavour. PA wants to give to the world, the world within and show the abundances of our lives. We all ride, "the ride of life" from different points, perspectives, spectrum, but all travel to the heart, the centre of "what life is to Penny Authors".

The collections in these books you will feel and experience experiences that will take you in and out, emotionally, mentally and spiritually. All you have to do is allow yourself get on a ride that will become a merry-go-round then may turn to a roller coaster ride, it will take you through life of all ages and some be it familiar experiences and occurrences, and to some an out of this world or weird and something wonderful.

We at Penny Authors like to recognise, remind and remember all the Penny Authors that have taken part, past always and present and you can find the full list in the books and now we have our website where all poets published through PA have their own profile page, thus achieving our original goal. The following list is to include and introduce the newcomers who are featured in this volume and are now listed on-line. They bring with them refreshing and unique life they've lived for us to read, enjoy and experience; each to their own take. The newcomers are listed on the "Roll Call":

This is the tenth instalment of the "Book of Lived," that lets you live life along with yours. If you would like to get involved then email us on pennyauthors@yahoo.co.uk and visit our website: www.pennyauthors.org.uk for updates and what's happening. So see you on the other side.

This is the 3rd year where "Book of Live" has no names beside the poems, to the reader, no prior influences of the writer, nationality, gender or creed, culture or customs. All poems are presented equally, without identity attached, but just one voice. This experience tests you and your tolerance, your difference, you can gauge your spirit, how open you are.

Finally, we hope you will enjoy reading the Book of Lived.

Roll Call

We at Penny Authors like to recognise, remind and remember all the Penny Authors that have taken part past always and present:

1.   Mayar Akash (Founder)
2.   Zainab Khan,
3.   Paul Harvey,
4.   Isaac Harvey,
5.   Rebekah Vaughan,
6.   Rabia Mehmood,
7.   Tamanna Parveen,
8.   Ellis Dixon-King,
9.   Liam Newton,
10.   Professor Muhammad Nurul Huque,
11.   Kalam Choudhury,
12.   Rashma Mehta,
13.   Mathew Saunders Whiting
14.   Akik Miah
15.   Nirmal Kaur
16.   Julie Archbold
17.   Lora Ashman
18.   John Robert Gordon
19.   Julie Anne Wheeler
20.   Late Joan Hodge
21.   Ruth Lewarne
22.   Bhupendra M. Gandhi
23.   Nicki & Laura Ellis
24.   Alga Statham
25.   Jeremy J. Lovelady
26.   Peter Fox
27.   Jamal Hasan
28.   Stephan Goldsmith
29.   Clare Saunders Whiting
30.   Sally Walker
31.   Elsa Kiernanfox
32.   Jaida Begum
33.   Abdul Mannan
34.   John Cynddylan Dillon
35.   Suzette Reed
36.   Sandra Sanjeet Green
37.   Coral Dodsworth
38.   Amitrajit Raajan

39. Chris York
40. Ossian Hughes
41. Stuart Cooper
42. Mustak Mustafa
43. Samiul Fox
44. Ayesha Chowdhury
45. Ferdous Rahman
46. Abu Maryam Gous
47. Steve Willoughby
48. Abul Hussain
49. Libby Pentreath
50. Paul Phillips
51. Adrian Smith
52. Paul Crump
53. Roger Lowry
54. Moriom Chaudhury
55. David Harley
56. John S. Wallis
57. Michael Ashton
58. Sabina Begum
59. Mary Fletcher
60. Rob Kersley
61. Tyrone M Warren
62. Alison Ali Norton
63. Andrew Harry
64. Janey Bryson
65. Paul Keeting
66. Res John Burman
67. Robyn Harry
68. Jade Carter-Bennet
69. Leo Rudman
70. Opu Islam
71. Eve Wakeling
72. Edwin Lewis
73. Tahi Chowdhury
74. Jenny Bishop
75. Angie Butler
76. Adrian Frost
77. Vivian Pedley
78. Robert Spencer
79. Pam Turner
80. Leema Begum
81. Chloe Hall

82. Keith Woodhouse
83. Alan S Whitfield
84. Sonja Fairfield
85. Daniel Munn
86. Penny Collins
87. Julie Flowerdew
88. Rosie Beale
89. Carol Bea
90. Ruth Husbands
91. Neil Graham Oats
92. Joanna Edwards
93. Antony Craig Oats
94. Bea Thompson
95. Nayma Chumchoun
96. Jonathan Hayter
97. Mukut Borpujari
98. Francesca Owen
99. Lowenna Helen Kaute
100. Valerie Kaute
101. Christine Jilbert
102. Nicole Paton
103. Errol Powel
104. Graham Rhodes
105. Mary Elizabeth Down
106. Gary Curson
107. Derrick J Hardy
108. Keith Lesser
109. Matthew Hill
110. Thomas Derek Lynas
111. Loretta Gray
112. Jack Bennet
113. Sarah Turner

For more information or if you would like to submit your work for inclusion, email: pennyauthers@yahoo.co.uk or visit our website: www.pennyauthors.org.uk

Love Is All That Exists

Do you know the love of all?
It's the whisper of the wind through the trees
The dance of sunlight on a rippling stream
The laughter of a child chasing after dreams

It's the bloom of a flower in the morning light
The embrace of a friend on a dark, lonely night
The warmth of a fire on a cold winter's day
The beauty of a sunset as it fades away

It's the joy in moments of simple delight
The strength found in standing up for what is right,
The peace of a quiet, starlit night
The hope that fills the morning light

Do you know what the love of existence is
It's the magic that surrounds us every day
In every smile, every tear, every kiss
In every heartbeat, in every way

So let us cherish this love that we share
In the beauty of life, in the moments we care
For in the end, it's all that we truly possess
The love of existence, our greatest success.

Rees Mogg

Like a pubic hair on a toilet seat
You really piss me off
Like a doctor in a hernia ward
You make me want to cough

Like a chameleon on a tartan rug
You never show true colours
Like wrist watch on a businessman
You've got no time for others

Like a violinist in a folk group
You're always on the fiddle
Like a double ended yo-yo
You play both ends against the middle

Like the eyes of the executioner
Peering from his mask
Like a piece of spat out chewing gum
You're sticking to your task

Like a one legged man in an arse kicking race
You're next to fucking useless
Like Sherlock Holmes in a Cluedo game
You're absolutely clueless

Like two lovers on a moonless night
You're groping in the dark
Like Frankenstein's monster on the slab
You're missing a vital spark

Like a dyslexic agnostic
That doesn't believe in Dog
You're stuck in the wrong century
Cos you're Jacob William Rees Mogg

The House In The Woods

The house
in the woods
that nobody knows
that nobody sees
except those
that know it's there.

And they are
the very people
you never, ever
want to meet
in or out
of the woods.

Aunty Mabel

Aunty Mabel's on the crack pipe,
a rat nest's voodoo Virgo,
and now I stand
In cloud cuckoo land,
Sailing on the sea.

Bog roll doggeroll,
the kings of scorpio,
I've numbered one
I've numbered two,
there's a place in my brain for you.

My Perfect Birthday

A slight twinkle of sun shining
through the gaps of the blinds.
The calming sound
of the curious baby birds singing through.

It's here, it's here, IT'S HERE!
you shout out
unable to contain the excitement.

The sweet scent of the freshly cut grass
sifting through the crack in the window,
entwining with the appetising scent of freshly baked bread,
as you slowly start to head down for breakfast
the sound of restrained laughter slowly starts to quiet.

POP!

The sound almost jumps into your heart
as confetti starts to fall,

Surprise!

Happy birthday!

And the last of the contained laughter bursting out,
the day passes like the smooth summer breeze,
blurring together
into one big ball of happy memories.

Today truly was my perfect birthday
you think to yourself
as you slowly drift to sleep

Abandoned

The whistle of the wind through the hair of the trees,
the sharp yet hollow hoot of the owl in the distance,
the warm gaze of sunlight peeking through the shrubbery,
thorns knotting around the remnants of the stone wall,
slowly crumbling into dust.

A scent of mud from the spring
slowly trickling into the nothingness,
the family of finches slowly gathering sticks
for their nest to survive the winter,
drip drip drip...
slowly getting slower
slowly getting colder
slowly becoming absent,
goodnight.

The spring dawn peeking through
the bare fingers of the trees,
slowly melting the cold glare of winter
as the morning has come,
crack the cheeps of baby finches
breaking free of their shells
calls the start of a new beginning.

This is my story
showing that nothing is ever
truly abandoned.

Elaborate Beauty

The glistening ocean
and the sparkling waves
almost taunting the winter,
dancing in its own world of absolute serenity.
The solid yet flowing sand rolling
and churning in a struggle to settle.

The free
yet somehow entrapped in a glow of cold beauty,
the sun glistening through the layers
of glowing snow,
the wind twisting and twirling around you,
dancing through the air
caressing your warmth,
your thought seem to stop
as the beauty of the world around you
slowly perforates your vision
you grasp onto this subtle warmth
the tide slowly drifts away,
the waves slowly waving goodbye
almost as if you would never see it again
as your mind drifts into slumber,
the world around you seems to stop.

This is my description of a place
I would find beautiful
through the perspective of a blank mind.

Dusk

The corpse ridden battle field
almost silent in despair,
the ringing of weapons clashing
can almost still be heard echoing
through the fog,

the grass dyed red
the sky growing ever darker
signalling the end of the horrors,

the stench overwhelming
as the crows caw in delight,
darkness drawing nearer
as the lost hopes of young soldiers disperse,
the carpet of blood
has finally come to a rest.

The Moors

The top moor
is deserted.
A wind scourers
Bending the trees
into skeleton shapes.
Skeins of wool
hang off
the pitiless gorse.
The clouds scurry
over the distant hills.
Tonight it is going to rain.

The Omniphiles Prayer

Bury me, my eyes, so I can see this land forever
in the depths of earth, where visions linger
let my sight be one with the roots that bind
to witness the beauty of this land, intertwined

Bury me, my hands, so I can touch this land forever
in the warmth of earth, where roots disperse
where life expands in glorious array
to feel the music of this land, its eternal pulse

Bury me, my ears, so I can listen to the songs of this land forever
in the silence of soil, where whispers echo
let melodies flow through the soil's embrace
to hear the harmonies of this land, in endless grace

Bury me, my voice, so I can sing the praises of this land forever
in the stillness of ground, where echoes reside
let my words blend with the earth's ancient hum
to lift my songs for this land, till kingdom come

Bury me, my heart, so I can love this land forever
in the quiet of earth, where feelings rest
let my love seep into the soil's embrace
to cherish the soul of this land, in eternal quest

Bury me deep, in the bosom of this land
where my essence merges with its very core
for in death, I find a timeless bond
to love, to sing, to listen, to see, forevermore.

Do You?

Do you feel the love, the love of everything
In the world
In the sea
In the womb of an unborn child
In the landscape flora and fauna and wonders of humanity
In the universe

'I do' whispers the breeze in the blue-bell wood
performing a symphony of fragrant chimes

It's a symphony of love,
A tapestry woven with threads of connection
That bind us to each other and to the world around us.
In the whispers of the wind
And the dance of the waves
In the laughter of a child
And the embrace of a friend
Love is the heartbeat of existence
Pulsing through the veins of creation

'I do' roars the wave, foaming wall of salty sparks
Embracing the shore with a hissing cry
'I do', 'I do' the eddies echo
retreating into eternal rhythm

From the smallest seed
To the grandest galaxy
Love is the force
That propels us forward
Guiding us through the dark
And illuminating the path ahead
It's in the blooming of a flower
And the song of a bird
In the laughter of a stranger
And the tears of a loved one

'I do' thunders the cloud
Flashing claws raking the hilltops
Splintered trees bow in quicksilver torrents
Do you feel the love,

cont.

The love that surrounds us
In every moment
In every breath
In the beauty of a sunset
And the stillness of the night
Love is the thread that weaves
Through the fabric of our lives
Binding us together
In a tapestry of light

I feel it in the breath of a mite
I feel it in the turbulence of a butterflies wingbeat
I feel it in the pull of a distant galaxy
I feel it in the heartbeat of an unborn child

So let us open our hearts
To the love that flows
Through all of creation
And let us be the vessels
Through which love shines
Brighter and stronger
Than ever before
For in the end
Love is all we have
And all we need.

Lucy

I'll call you when I wake up
you'll be putting on your make up
we'll talk about what we can see,
but you and I will never be.
Never dead, never free,
in this age of dark uncertainty.
I wanted her so badly I couldn't move,
she said: "it's right, we've got nothing to prove."

The Dream

In the quiet stillness of the night,
the dream hovers, uncertain,
as if seeking its missing creator,
a whisper in the wind

Once vivid and vibrant,
now faded and dim,
the dream struggles to hold on,
to memories of its origin,

What happens to the dream
When the dreamer leaves?
Does it linger in the shadows,
or drift away on a sigh?

The echo of the dreamer's laughter,
the warmth of their touch,
slowly dissipate,
leaving the dream adrift,

Yet still, it lingers,
a ghost of what once was,
a reminder of the beauty,
that once danced in the mind,

So the dream waits,
patiently biding its time,
hoping for the return
of the dreamers Light,

Is it not lifted up,
carried aloft, unseen,
by us who wonder, hope and wish.
We who also dream?

For that moment of reunion,
the dream will awaken once more,
and together they will create,
a world of endless possibility

London

With a mind full of doggeril,
like a used up toilet roll,
I try to toss off a poem,
a poem with no home,
too much upstairs,
too many nightmares,
I'm walking the touchstone
twixt truth and deceiving.
The universe is against me,
making it rain,
but there's only one reality,
and that's in my brain.
I want to live in London,
I think the city's ace,
when all's said and done
it might just fit my face,
get a green Mohawk,
talk jive talk,
change the way I walk,
linear lines line up in my mind,
no-one knows the situation,
thoughts are all you will find,
down in king's cross station.
Women have taken over my actions,
belonging to different factions,
it's 4.30, I'm feeling dirty,
got to see a man called Birty,
about some gear,
take away the fear,
hey baby come here,
I need to see your nips
I love your shapely hips,
sex has reared its ugly head,
it looks like we're going to bed,
I'm hideous but I got some bread,
one day we'll both be dead,
so let's get it together
in any kind of weather
bird's of a feather,
whatever whatever
Never say never
For ever and ever.

The Dawntreader

The ice was cropping over the lizard,
like a red-faced, white-bearded wizard,
his eyes ran circles round my skull,
the patchwork lace has faded dull.

The hills all bouncing green,
valleys split open a nascent seam,
the berries pupil red,
laser beams around my head.

White clusters of stalactites,
white sound that drenches the senses,
in all my eyes and ears it bites,
blackbirds lined up on fences.

Blind and searching numbly,
she comes over all comely,
I shine throughout the land,
I died by my own hand.

Lion

Your tail long and curling
Your claws sharp and clinging
Your teeth pointed and biting
Your eyes huge and staring.
Your mouth open and frightened.
Your body as heavy as an elephant.

But

Lion you are brave
Lion you are as gentle as a dove.

Time slip-the house where you no longer live

Written down in rings of wood, their keenness speaks again,
yells notice me, your birth, my death, my first of flowering bud,
and grape and pear and cherry grown now planted in your ground,
as weekly, daily, soil you trod, your laugh my speaking sound.

We sit and talk, like you once did, on seats spread all around,
and conversation round and round, your laugh my childhood sound.
The blooms unfold from your deep earth, come notice me again,
the clouds and sun seem still the same, the gentle sounds of rain.

Leaves dark and glossy, hard and soft, some struggle to live on,
their beauty slowly fading, their flowering nearly done,
like us in darker days to come, when life has passed us by,
when others tread these rocky paths and pause and think, and sigh.

Our legacy in word and deed, in bricks and mortar last,
our hopes for hearts held dear, and memories of the past.

Bee

My big broad smile fell into the Long thin
stems of green a multitude of vibrant sun kissed petals in bloom. Kindness glides
across my blades what cuts the finger
feeds the eye with beauty. Warm beams lightly caresses each petals the sweet
smell in the breeze like soft kiss's
bees with yellow baskets in flight
heading for the hive with delights pleased
will be the queen of the hive the bees job is to make honey and keep the queen
alive
and will thrive in the hive
being the queen of her tribe.

Darkness

Darkness distorts the mood on this day, that day,
is it the moon and the stars, these tides of emotion
that rattle rooms in anger,
come into lives, uncover lies?

The fun filled days of light leave, hasty to be gone, letting
discord flow like white hot lava, leaving destruction and despair,
glowing, consuming, overcoming everything in its path.
Our watery bodies weep and flow on these tides of despair,
walk a fine line, a tight rope, a binding thread,
as a buzzing fly flails broken in the spiders web.

The tame dog begets the howling wolf, its impacts raw,
and undeniable, shocking, unbelievable.
The worm turn sin the blink of an eye.
This eye for an eye becomes
a torment of anger, a battle of words
hurled without reason, dragged
from the past to distort and change the future.

Or is there another way?

A Rainy Night

Outside
the rain falls.
Bouncing across the tarmac.
Blurring the yellow lines.
A man
turns up his collar,
and walks faster.
Bad weather for the street cats,
that stops their prowling,
hiding under shelter,
under sheds
behind walls.
Tonight even the rats
will stay home.

Carousel

There are slabs of time in which I am framed as lopsided,
I walk forward into the landscape of the past,
it's an unknown territory to my forward pointed shape,
a body through time,
thought is time,
memory frames experience with broken promises and lies,
it promises more of the same,
roundabout of experience,
serves the same and same again,
a carousel of sadness,
faces warped by gravity,
laughter drowned with tears.

Time Goes by So Fast

Sometimes it's better not to remember
Sometimes it's better to forget
Sometimes it's better just to turn the page
And wipe away the debt
Nostalgia ain't what it used to be
Don't look back with sorrow
When all is finally said and done
Today will be yesterday tomorrow
Time is what you make it
It's never on your side
Between the living and the dead
Is where two worlds collide
So always live for tomorrow
And don't dwell in the past
Cos when you're getting older
Time goes by so fast
And one day you'll be called Spiderman
Cos you can't get yourself out of the bath.

The World Is Beautiful

This world is so beautiful...
Made up of lands and water...
There is nothing you could ever imagine...
Back to reality you could see everything with your own eyes...
Eyes open wide and sense everything at the same time...
There are sea, land, gravity, air, clouds in many different shapes...
Once you stand up and see everything that reflect in you...
amazing!

What else could you see?...
Animals, wildlife and humans!
Indeed so many creators out there...
The whole universe with several planets and galaxy...
This world a planet is where everything grows and lead to a life with so many creators...
There is a hidden world out there where we could not see in our eyes...

We are speechless... there is so many planets out there that exist...
be grateful you got to see everything and don't waste your precious life in this world.

The whole universe created by the only one god
god is almighty!

Xmas Card Painting

Anthony Frost's Xmas card from the far southwest of Cornwall
to his brother in the northwest Ozarks of Arkansas

"...nothing I cared about in the lamb-white days that time would take me
Up in the swallow-thronged loft by the shadow of my hand
In the moon that is always rising
Nor that riding to sleep
I should hear him fly with the high fields
And wake to the farm forever fled from the childless land
Oh, as I was young and easy
Time held me green and dying
Though I sang in my chains like the sea..."

My brother Anthony Frost made this beauty of a painting
in his studio which is about a paintbrush
Throw away from where the poet Dylan Thomas who wrote
the above poem married Caitlin
In Penzance a little long time ago

Breakrock

Isotope and artefact, prototype and example,
the meadow curves like a vibrant temperature,
her curves match mine in a lesser listening,
and the forked cove spreads out unbuttoned,
stems of roses hook through the hooded cave,
and higher up the cliff forkening stems curve.

Perfidious mountains where sheep and cattle
are extolled in the mirrored beginning of god's command,
jumbled the madness of the weather's occult mind,
as easy slow kids vowel blue and red syllables
and all about this fermenting land thinks a happening man,
I couldn't but temperately give you no wishes.

The Glow

Sympathetic resonance
& compassionate actions
which are in fact the deepest
teachings.
Setting aside time
to schedule grief
a selfish act
because fatalities keep me hidden.
Once more falling to the feet
of the ritual
by accepting the predictability that comes with it.
The smell of Exotic fevers,
muscle spasms
& weeping wounds
that glisten in the warm light of day.
Yellowish eyes stare back blankly while secretly harbouring fantasies
of romance & companionship
from pale faces with nosebleeds who tell
tales out of school
with their thin wet lips
that resemble
slash marks.

Ahh the glow of charisma
the art of longing
for the detested & despicable
(voyeuristic energy)
& the enclosed garden.
Do you have the capacity
to forget how uncomfortable
you are when the hyenas
come to town
to chap on your door?
Warrior configuration
through silent vocation.
Fear not,
If it moves the magi will interpret it.
Leap & the net will appear
because there's a silent thread that weaves
through the fabric of all our timelines.

Invisible Projects

Born from Dark Hearts in Ivory towers
who impose & dictate their
dogmas & propaganda
from up above.
Dupers delight
the allure of narcissism & delusion
In search for the ultimate freedom.
The ethics of intimacy
discussed from the safety nets of echo chambers.
A state of unease & the absence of reality underpins it all.
Bear witness as a new morning dawns
the secret teachings unleashed
via the tabloids & spreadsheets.
The outpouring of neuroses
& trauma the faucet is dripping
the tap is running
an emotional ejaculation
in a public space
in the public's eye!

The dark erotica has arrived
as a new day dawns
& casts its shadow over all dominion.
The pariahs (individual thought) are the new witches to be despised
& burnt at the stake
via rumours & character assassinations.
As worshippers
kneel & rejoice at the altar
of the State.

The Maze Of Your Mind

Entering the labyrinth of life
is it left for a degree
and right for a knife?
Straight ahead for a dead end
or around the corner for a wife?

Are you meant to
push through the gap
in order to hedge your bets?
Or doomed to wander the maze
until the end of your days?

Or would you want to have a map
tucked away beneath your cap,
explaining it was just
a lucky turn or two,
that won the prize for you?

Or would you watch others and learn
from their every twist and turn
hanging back as they retreat,
following the patter of their feet
and if the goal heaves into sight,
push them aside with all your might
holding the prize,
above their jealous eyes?

Or are you the intellectual
who knows that wandering blindly
is totally ineffectual
and that reason must be your guide.
Who would plan a quest
where the idiot did the best?

No, the thinker,
would know a proper maze
must by its intention,
have many wandering ways
that seeking to avoid the prize
is where the true path lies.

cont.

Whether you shout or laugh or weep
or if you are noble, a bully or a cheat
matters not to the maze of life.

It's only the maze within your mind
that sometimes can be quite unkind.

Sitting With Chickens

It's always Sunday and time is slow.
She is up early and heads out for walk
before the world awakes
and moves around the streets.

Back home they linger over breakfast,
fruit and toast, chew over the needs
of the store cupboard and the day.
Have we got eggs? On their lips again.

Her childhood self remembers
back yard chickens to feed,
the smell of warm bran,
the warmth of their settled bodies.

The biblical names, her priest father gave them.
Cardinal, her favourite, large, white, would squat,
allow the girl to pick her up and stroking her bony wings,
she'd sit amongst contented clucking.

The times collude to bring back memories,
a yearning to turn back seventy years,
to feel again the timeless joy
of sitting with chickens.

Hotel Comforts

In semi-darkness
Your head and shoulders
Are half a jigsaw puzzle piece
Lying in the slumbrous comfort
Of a hotel

Who would not love a wonderfully
Bland and comfortable hotel?
The bed so soft,
An under quilt beneath our heavy bodies
The walls taupe
The time a small turquoise glowing number
Massive lamps
Free emblazoned pens
Temperature controlled
Hot water that cannot scald
Peppermint tea
Breakfast buffet in a vast array
Mirrored lifts that glide us
Protection from the busy, grimy, raucous struggle.

This how the rich, the famous, live
Cosseted

Blanketed
Cocooned
Travelling in taxis cheerfully enough through
Lashing rain, intoxicating heat
Never folding their nightclothes
Never cleaning their bathrooms
Which greet them returned to
Immaculate shining splendour
After a satisfying breakfast
Soothed
How can they see the poor
Even the ordinary working people
As more than a movie passing
Unfortunates, represented as if by actors
Not touching them, not, unless they remember
Once not being rich

cont.

Once not having it easy
And are empathetic

I rolled up my bus window quick
That time in Delhi
Keeping a leprous finger out
Disgust and fear rising
So it is to the rich
Poverty could be catching.

Drawn to Black

His black suit,
cloak and robes
looked to the child's brown eyes.

She saw love in the black
of his clothes,
took his colour as her own.

The black of his pen, his writing,
taught her to seek
the same black upon the page.

Her brush chose to canvas dark
her walls, black smelled of her father,
smokey safe.

His hand guided hers,
his colours became her future.
She was always drawn to black.

Rainsong

Gusty, driving, summer rain
how you relieve me of my pain!
How you make me think of trees,
paper boats and sulking toads;
the pain of the empty harbour at noon!
The fretful, scowling wind,
you weave a chant that creates a hole
in my heart;
and in your ardour high and proud,
makes me shout and laugh out loud!

Summer rains that start at dawn,
dropping veils of saddest moan,
seeping water between wet grasses,
sweeping dirt from leaves in masses,—
smearing, blurring out the distant past,
in a dream you hold me fast;
scolding, urging to let go
things that are, for things that are yet to be.

Torrential, hurling rain at night
hurtling down with might and gait,
you but make me hug my sheet,
fondly sheltered from your teeth.
Now I woo my crackling fire,
piling, piling drift-wood higher.
Kith and kins and pictures old
hearten while you heave and toil!

Pelting, melodious showers of spring
force me to remember
olden times and gleeful too,
small joys and heart-breaks true,—
fond memories I'd silently rue,
were not oblivious and sadder yet.
Ah! you twist my bosom with pain,
gleeful, resonant April rain!

Summer rain,
how you make my heart grew fond!
Whistling, gleeful showers of spring,
how I love the pain you bring!

Bullseyes

Big bulls eye bulging round black slates
nailed with irons and screwed down to red plates
Watching from the dry dusty brown field over that broken gate
Seven miles as the cow flies to its nearest watch,
looking is the lady from her window box.
Stealth as the vole scurries by the hidden rock down the rabbit's hole to find its
family cosy in a flock.

The fly on the wall listen's with heavy wings
the sound of secrecy how much does it bring
How much does it weigh do we know anyway
or how deep is its depth
do those floors have trap doors, tell me more

The elephant stands big and tall in the corner if the room
no-one knows where it went
no-one no1 at all
no one wants to talk
be honest or vent

The lepers spots have faded with scars of battle
untold lesson learn from young passed on to old
Fork tongue silently observes its pray
empty tummy hurting
he needs to eat today.

Coloured Threads

The coloured threads
of life's spinning wheel
start slowly, gathering speed,
the colours merge and change,
as each backward view
becomes clear.

The pace changes,
in slow motion,
as we, with measured breath, watch
strangling strands,
thin as spider's silk,
barely visible over the years,
become knotted, twisted,
ever tighter they weave
around the two of us.

Surrounded,
you begin the change.
And as you fly
above life's wheel
you leave me
clinging to the empty
shell of sadness.

The Grey Dog

The grey dog of discontent continues
to bark up the wrong tree,
flinches at shadows and pulls harshly,
then lurches towards others,
cowers distractedly, when faced with a fiercer foe.
Is he barking up the wrong tree again,
not seeing the wood for the trees?
His daily walks frustrate many, as here again he stops,
looks up, barks,
and barks, and waits,
then sniffs around and rubs his back against this one's smooth bark.
It feels good, this one.
But is it good enough?
There are plenty more to gain his attention it is true.
But this one bends its branches,
shelters him in the heat of the sun,
the driving rain of tears of loss,
its lush leaves
weave a healing dappled pattern on his aging skin,
he barks again,
we wait, and hear his whining in our darkening days.

This Month I Dwell On Water

This month I dwell on water,
draw from it my experience, my well.
    The ice of it, slippery, its ruining lives.
The cold shiver of death as it slithers down your back,
making you shake, and its snap like a heart that breaks.
    The quench of it, when the tears stop their travelling path
from eyes to chin, their healing sadness filled
by a glass of life giving flow, water,
giving back through colourless draught, the loss of pain
taken hungrily sip by healing sip.
    The warmth of it, in cup held hand, shared with a loving friend.
In scalding shower, when muscles ease and movement
freshed and flesh revealed, relieved of daily grime and toil.
    The vast of it, in seas of salt to match those tears of human pain,
of endless, shortened life, and endless death, reflections puddled in the rain,
that too must fall from sunny skies, to shout the truth of life not lies.
    Not lies of how to win a pound, but laughter, friendship, growing land,
these mixed with dirt to make a mud, to build a life so solid- good.

    That is my dwell on water now,
that life is like a kind of soup and sorrows poured
and mixed, to make a healing life,
of friends and good times mixed with bad,

these can really help you, when you're feeling sad.

Round Here

Round here
there's a price
for everything
and everyone has
a price.

Round here
every days
an adventure
in a nightmare
paradise.

Round here
The cats use
broken bottles
and the rats
all carry knives.

Round here
the pigeons spread
false rumours
and neighbours
spread their lies.

Round here
we try to
carry on
whilst keeping
carrying on.

Round here
we sit here
waiting
for the fat lady
to finally sing her song.

I believe (Liz Truss)

I believe that all in wrestling
Isn't fixed
I believe that magic's always real
And not just tricks
I believe the Met Police
Never ever fail
I believe all the stuff that's
written in the Mail
I believe when Jesus
calls us all a bunch of sinners
and when the bookie says he's happy
paying out the winners
I believe when the dentist
Says it isn't going to hurt
I believe it's really camping
Staying in a Yurt
I believe that Leeds Untied
will win the cup
I believe that a pint of
John Smiths is fit to sup
I believe it when a banker
Says my accounts important
I believe it when they tell me
My loo papers absorbent
I believe that Winnie the Pooh
Is really very sinister
But I can't believe Liz Truss
Will be our next Prime Minister

This One's For Jackie Overfield

The sunsets in the background
Behind the Lowfield stand
Factory chimneys on horizons
When the fans all left by tram
The fifties when all our teams
Played in black and white
Homemade scarves and wooden rattles
In smoggy, gas-light nights
The ghosts of players lost in time
echo round the final whistle.
Their game is done, their boots are hung
there's no one left to listen
to the names, the fans all chanted
the names from old team sheets
Don Revie, Jimmy Ashall,
Grenville Hair and Georgie Meek,
Noel Payton, Billy Humphries,
Jackie Overfield and Chris Crowe.
Archie Gibson, Jackie Charlton,
and Ted Burgin in the goal.
Their names are carved on gravestones
Somewhere in this land
But their fame lives on forever
in hearts of old Leeds fans
whose lives too, soon will end,
when there'll be no one left to say
they were standing in the Scratching Shed
and saw Jackie Overfield play.

Slaying of a White Pigeon

A White Pigeon
flying across the horizons
spreading peace-
exhausted, torn and relentless.
reached the skyline of Gaza.
White shrouds of lifeless corpses beneath
like fallen white feathers awaiting
to be buried deep down.
They dreamt of White Pigeons
soaring high in the blues.

The sky turned dark with smoke of gunpowder, burnt air.
Scattered limbs of White Pigeon
dripping fresh blood on Tel Aviv.
A torn wing tumble upon 10 Downing Street
and the other falls in the White House.
Tettered head hurled towards
the European Union,
Abdomen full of wastes wings it way to Arab.
Lower back toppled in the UN
and the rest of limbs descended in some lands.

They're all peace keeper of the world.
They adorned flowers on their lapels
and carry weapons behind the scenes.
They offer aids with one hand and drench another with blood.
They reverse the role: snake and shaman!

They will paint their own canvases,
fiddle with the fictitious White Pigeon!
They sow the seed of deception in disguise,
call it 'Peace'...
Sigh! Violence, destruction and death prevail.

The Waltz

Scarlet scarves as nooses
protrude crudely from pale limp necks with swollen blue tongues.
Resembling a grotesque exotic orchid with an odd permutations
(suspended in animation)
a poor lapse in judgment
for onlookers to see.

The humiliation ritual
is a common day occurrence
& the currency of favour for empty
vessels devoid of respect & self-worth.

**The shame will be incoming
with a vulgar display of power**

The band plays on for the waltz to arrive.
Witness the morbid mockery
as dissociation takes you by the hand for this transaction to begin.
Humiliation for commerce
as the receipts run their mouth
& big up their chest!

**The shame will be incoming **

with a vulgar display of power
like the drone strike at a middle Eastern wedding on that fateful afternoon
(a disgusting show of force documented for life)

As guilty parties barter with broken promises & empty gestures
like sign language for the blind.
**The shame will be incoming
when the receipts run their mouth with a vulgar display of power!

Why protest about Gaza?

Lunching in a cafe
I tell the young man at the next table
I'm going to a demonstration
Calling for a ceasefire in Israel
Bombing Gaza to pieces.

He says now he's older
He no longer does this sort of thing
What can it enable?

At the demo we hear the history
A Palestinian tells us a 9 year girl
Wrote a will to leave her few shekels
As she expects to die
The crowd listens in silence
Some moved to cry.

We want to know we did what we could
We joined in global protest
We defied our mad Suella Tory ruler
Who calls us hate filled,
When we're full of love
People you don't normally hear
Stood on a wall with a loud hailer
We won't be silent
Justice and Peace our aim
And next week we will turn up
Just the same.

Perpetual Parlance

We parlez on the playa,
A liquescent blue rhapsody
tablecloth with fluttering white trim.
Beyond the cobblestoned pier,
La vie de la mer,
Beyond what the eye sees.
The air laced with grilled sardine,
Pierced by the scream
of the lifeguard's whistling ire.

A jalaba tanned figure unfurls his mat
On the sand, facing East-Southeast,
His hands raised to his head.
You beam with the brilliance of the sun,
like the sea the moment brims and runs
Into the horizon and mountains crowned in mist,
Our words swallowed by the seabed
as the waves curled and crashed.

A rainbow ocean of palpitating parasols
Greet an angel blue sky,
Streaks of gold and silver clutch the sunlight.
Polished by the sand's rough,
The world is more than enough,
Its troubles breezily pass us by
There is no darkness when the sun holds back the night
and summer's sojourn cups the buds of the soul.

We playfully parlez
as the children run and splash,
Their squeals of delight
Cutting through the air
before finding our ears,
Our words fissure and alight,
Card games and cigarette ash,
Warm plastic cups of atay.

You fish for seashell keepsakes
from the resting, baking grains,
The heat paints our salty limbs,

cont.

Your chiselled shoulders
glisten and smoulder.
When the dream wakes only shells remain
and our voices in the sea's basin
where the spell never breaks.

Matchead

Words are words,
words are all there is,
nothing exists except words.
words continue and words connect,
it is the word,
language is all we can believe in.

What is the language using us for?

We are words,
action is pure,
but it becomes language,
nothing exists except words,
poetry is the right words in the right order.

Moonshine Doves

Split from the mountain domes,
when my wife lends me her puckered lips,
the yellow split ends of pine planks
meekly take the planes sharp edge,
obsessed with my needs and desires,
I throw a big bucket of garbage all over the lawn.

Time is bashing in my skull,
autumn stains my blood,
the whole planet curves to a lull,
the seas grow huge and flood
the world the size of a frozen pea
spins out of orbit and descends
a thousand universes of time and space,
to lie with the one god's beautiful face
and leave all murder far behind.

Orange 10

You know I'd like to meet you,
like to be introduced,
I'd like to smell your feet you,
get you all juiced.

I saw you through the crowded room,
saw you at the bar,
you make my head go boom
you never wear a bra.

You're always with your friends,
I can't get a look in,
the story never ends,
you just so damn good looking.

My mates tell me,
I don't have a chance,
but if you could just shoot me,
that one special glance.

Living My Best Life

I wasn't the one who missed out there...
Lucky escape I reckon.
Things happen for a reason,
I do not doubt that for a second.
Things worked out well for me,
Now I'm in a happy place.
So, looking back,
I'm glad you left,
I needed the time & space.
Now my life has changed dramatically,
And my world is good.
I told you I'd live my best life.
Because I always knew I could.

Paint Hotel

Cat out in back. lean the rhythm lunch,
spend think crash out,
leaning blacks a mouse sink in the gay rut.
Peach blind some score in
the who you done rain train of last but
easy riff clanger being spent night in
a closed hoof. important head will
reach as clash rash blurt burt sex
in a loud place.
Round goes the last knowledge.
blast from a sharp rock stoned derange blink
in a month call of water the naked land turn.
pink in clock the sky bent as lark puke and
sound sin rout john seems a bit little spark.
itch it blunt red nut notch spout pout
free the crag word of a sun point.

Ancestry

When I look in the mirror,
Thousands of faces made me me,
Every single ancestor,
Was involved with how I came to be.
I find out about each of you,
Who you were & how you lived,
Whereabouts you spent your time,
And some of the things you did.
And traits of personality,
Start to shine right through,
And I can see so clearly,
That I am a part of you.
So I honour each one of your presence,
And I thank you that I am here,
I want you to know that I think of you all,
In my heart you are so dear.

You're the best

In the busy buzz of life each day,
Take time for yourself, in your own way.
A warm bath,
 a book to read,
Self-care's the key,
for every need.

A hug,
a smile,
a gentle breeze,
Self-care and self-love,
bring us ease.

In each moment,
old and new,
Self-care and self-love,
help us renew.

So cherish yourself,
you're worth it all,

In self-care and self-love,
stand tall.

For when you nurture yourself,
you see,
You're the best you can be,
you'll see.

Growing Old as One

Side by side,
they've journeyed through the years,
from teenage dreams to adult fears.

Through ups and downs,
they've stayed strong,
together, they've danced life's song.

From school crushes to love's embrace,
they've grown together, found their place.

As time flies by, they hold each other near,
growing old together, without fear.

With every laugh line and every grey hair,
their love deepens, without compare.

Hand in hand, they face each day,
as they find life's winding way.

Growing old together, but never apart,
with love as their guide, and youth in their heart.

Together forever, whatever may come,
as they journey through life, their hearts beat as one.

Beyond Illsuions

In a world of flashy cars and designer brands,
where wealth seems to be all that demands,
we're led to believe that money's the key,
to happiness, success, and being carefree.

But behind the glitter and the shiny show,
lies a truth that's often let go.

For money can't buy the things that truly matter,
like love, friendship, or moments that scatter.

So don't be fooled by the illusion's shine,
for true richness is found in simpler times.

In laughter with friends and moments of glee,
that's where the real treasure will always be.

Milky Quartz Crystal 2014

Pyramidic, pegmatitic
Hard waxy lustre,
Brittle quartz shard,
Within splinter cluster.

Cave cracking line
Across crusted reef
Sloping, six-sided
Split silicon teeth

Fractured fissures deep
In cloudy composite,
Glinting milky light, where
Ghostly rainbows sit.

Black & White

Black and white
Thick and furry
Snuggly and affectionate,
big marble eyes
which glare into my own

The softest touch
when his paws dig into my skin
his gentle meows of hello,
and sweet purrs of love –

Brings some sort of comfort within
an unexplainable type.
those who tell me
"it's just a cat"
just don't understand

They don't know that
"Just a cat"
could bring such happiness
and friendship to oneself

They have no idea
of what kind of cuddles
"Just a cat" could give

They couldn't imagine
of the unconditional love of
"Just a cat"
have for their owners

The love he shows me
is much more than what words could even tell

What more could I possibly ask for?

Night Terrors

The abandonment wound has opened up again,
it's walls go deep into a darkness,
I have never seen,
a hole for ever open,
it lies staring at the sky, like some big black eye,
yet love transcends it's depths,
fashions it's walls,
there the blackness breathes;
some great monster,
I can hear it in the rising and falling of its breath,
for me, and for me, alone;
'those we love, and those who love us,
cannot come with us,'
it seems to whisper,
their hearts still beating,
an energy that keeps us from the darkness in us,
is no more, the guardrail gone,
the descent unaided,
no ropes to guide me,
just the sound of darkness heaving,
breathing,
is there no end to death in life
when all sorrow is washed out?
Each moment squeezed of every ounce of feeling,
night terrors that suffocate a colourless world,
breathing,
devoid of life, devoid of feeling,
as I lay awake in the early hours of another day...

Night Bus

I slipped off the night Bus,
like a creature of the night,
(and unused to the light),
the city stank of smoke, exhaust fumes, stale air,
shadows in the grey light of dawn pulled at my clothes,
as if someone else was in there?

'You have a good heart. But nobody knows!'
Henna stained hands pressed at my side,
'Come with us!' they cried!

Yet from somewhere deeper,
and hidden in a flat silence, a whirlpool of water opened inside me!
Watery twister,
storm clouds have gathered;
and a darkness has called me to its edge;
the whale- eye that glistened, had listened,
drunk on its tiredness, and with relentless motion,
it was suddenly 'all at sea',
then the whale eye spoke;
It spoke to me!
It told me of the valley beyond death,
as it lifted the veil,
and suspended my breath!

It opened; the gate to chaos!
And shared its dark mystery;
the bond that had opened between 'life and life',
whilst it whispered a forgiveness, and coveted uncertainty.
I was paralysed by its one eyed stare,
I waited as each watchful moment,
in its soft song it sung to me an unchained melody;
as if eternity were there!

I opened my eye,
the tears fell like stars from a firmament,
as the veil closed about me,
it captured my heart,
then new songs of dawn pushed me forward,
and into the bright light of a new day.

Dinosaur Bones

It was felt a vibration maybe how do you explain a look across a room
a wordless arrow flies and your copiousness
your concentration
your consciousness stirs into action
…traveling through a gulch at night
the rock walls call out the agony of their separation
the moon howls
the dinosaur bones buried in the desert sand
whisper their need of you tonight.

In the oceans Whale calls kiss fathoms deep
…a secret smoke signal of the heart goes up in a child's mind
and crosses the cryptic waves tumbling in the spindrift seas
lassoing cabbalas crystal hymns structured with cosmic song
situated in the human brain and in the mountains
stalagmiting caves gyringing the fire
the wood the metal the ice giving pouring rain

When I saw the albino footprint on the museums carpet floor
it was like a gong going off in a Tibetan hillside temple
no one had been here before…
unless the mark the turn of heel
the footprint was written in the cloth adepts of Oedipus
I looked at that mark like man Friday in the desert of my heart
my eyes turned to lasers and the making of my first movement caught fire
like nimrod I threw Abraham into the flames
but when I awoke the print was still there despite the flames
the mark of the past here in front of me for telling futures pain
I would rest it on your tongue
sweet soldier drink it into your look red veins
take it and spin it toe to toe
print to bring another's foot loose and fancy free a fools cap
burden not thee and in the waiting of the tidal turn right
on that Point in the orgasm of the estuary
pick that foot up,
and walk that sea.

D-Day

I sat on a bench in the sun
At a bus stop in St Ives
Surrounded by Germans

D -day commemorations
I suppose they know

None of us old enough to have been there
But our fathers fought each other
Some of theirs maybe Nazis

My mother-in-law
A child on Porthminster beach
When it was straffed

Now they come and see our town
No sign of hatred or dismay

But remembering Hitler
Had an eye on Zennor
for his post-war second home

How eighty years can change things
How lucky we
Who have not had to risk our lives
Or suffered war to now be free.

Tango

Takes two to tango

Well more because
You have to learn it
Even walking is all new
Something we thought
We knew how to do.

Then you have to be passed round
To find out how to follow
How to lead
So close together
But no close intent
The closeness came so quickly
Then it went
Then it's another
But no lust
It's just
The music and the moves
The rhythm
Three minutes and they're gone

But that night
Under the stars
A warm night
In Sardinia
With you
It was just us two
Dancing
In love
Forever

Toxic Spirituality

Is life really just a series
Of beautiful breakages,
Whose intricate patterns are
Seared with hot gold?
Or is that what we're told?

Striving for spiritual excellence,
Instead of being in the present.
A new spiritual masochism,
What's that all about?
A new trend, no doubt.

Why are we striving
For a life without meaning?
Navel-gazing ourselves
Into another dimension.
Are we hoping for ascension?

Why are we proselytising about
Clean living and enlightenment
Or on positive thinking?
Why should we strive for nirvana
Or go looking for prana?

Instead

Maybe realise that
humans are equal parts of
glamour and squalor.
And that life is messy, chaotic
balance of both raw and exotic

It's held together by
hope and arguments
and kindness, and danger.
There's no unbroken chain
(meet up in the next life again).

Nevertheless, it's a rich,
textured, nuanced life,
filled with equal parts
of dirt and desire.
Would-be fuel for our spiritual fire.

Could it be that we're just
addicted to escaping reality?
Which I heard doesn't exist, anyway.
Should we discuss it further, my friend?
No... I think it should end.

Heart Haiku

Heart ticks far too slow
thirty three beats per minute
head spins like a top.

Headaches aplenty
dull pressured thuds from within
fears I won't wake up.

Medication helps
pacemaker needed but still
two years on, I wait.

My doctor says there's
ectopic beats within my
bradycardia.

The consultant says
we are monitoring you
keep you updated.

Genuine question,
will I be dead by that time?
Will I qualify?

Zennor Field Trip

On a ragged, cliff top trail
winding on, seekers walk
on shoe-polished stone
and bleached grass stalk

Follow on, honeyed gorse
on the granite hedgerows
follow where the skylark pips
and the sweet honesty grows

Onward to the graveyard, now
where a weathered family grieved
now rested on the headstone
a rusted, feathered wreath

Now under breeze-swept blossom
I gladly find solace
once more into the 'tinner's arms'
in his warmly held embrace

With the dark rustic floorboards
and beer in plastic crates
the Paninis under parasols,
and pesto-covered plates.

The Solar Eclipse of the Sun

The purity of innocence is mine to rebirth
and I shall rekindle the flames
and heal planet earth
for the light of the truth
that burns brightly within
will release the fears of mankind
and free them from sin
for the heart speaks the truth
and how mighty the sword
drawn to serve mother earth
and sing with one beautiful voice
little bird, little bird soon to take flight
spread your beautiful wings
and let the world see your light
for the compassion of our love
sows new seeds of content
so that you may rebirth
and arise on wings heaven sent
to awaken those chosen
to carry the light
that the earth may be saved
from her struggle and plight
god speed angel of courage
head towards the sun
and may god's blessing be with you
when you meet the solar eclipse of the son.

Legacy

She was quite direct this time,
and seemed less concerned it might hurt.
Said I'm not my new haircut
and not this new season's tee-shirt.
And as for my labels,
and as for my slogans and words;
they are nothing but dust
in the down of the feathers of birds.

Invading my dreams she then
lectured me like a true friend.
Said I'm not the result,
and I'm not how my story will end.
In the hands of all others,
my voice could be mute as a mime.
It's the choices I make that define
what I am for all time.

She held out her hand, it was steady,
my fingers found hers.
Her voice knew my fear,
but her words formed the sweetest of verse.
She said, "love is painful".
I followed her lips as she talked,
"you will be your motives,
 you will be the path that you walked".

For a moment an echo
of Sunday school came into view.
Something about serpents, of Adam,
and his free will too.
But then just as quickly it faded
and all I could see,
was the core of an apple,
and the blessings and curse of a tree.

She might come again,
I don't know, but I'll wait each new moon.
Cos I may need reminding,
I might need some comforting soon.   cont.

If awareness is key,
then the child in me is afraid,
that my legacy won't be much more
than the choices I made.

My legacy won't be much more
than the choices I made...

Re-addressed

What I believed as I set out in life,
changed as the settings of life did.

What I saw then,
I don't see now.

How I saw things then,
don't now look the same.

Outlook, perception changes,
naivety topples
as we move with time.

What one once thought?
change shape and re-addressed.

Conflicted Coexistence

I would rather bad news from the honest,
than lies from a fool.
But I heard the smooth-tongued one,
the one they made lord of home rule
justifying supplying
yet more bombs to wipe from the face.
Indigenous families,
oppressed in
a western
disgrace.

Needing air, then.
I pumped up my tyres,
tears pooled in my eyes,
and out of the saddle I rode
under postcard blue skies.
Late spring had brought swallows and martins
and colours aglow.
Precious acts of defiance in joy,
sweeping down Nancherrow.

Kelynack... Trevascan... Polgigga,
each ley line ingrains
sweet salt from the air
and the birdsong's cacophonic strains.
Then climbing from Gulval,
Nancledra stays hidden from view.
But the sweep of mount's bay makes me gasp
as I breathe what is true.

Through Cripplesease, Zennor and Morvah,
round each ancient bend.
The sun and the headwind,
as apothecaries might send,
to forge triumphs from trials,
young bruises each mother has kissed.
Conflicted, the entities;
beauty and pain
coexist.

It's Complicated

The man in the picture has had his face buried
in the blanket which covers the small bodies.
From beneath the blanket
I can only see one blood stained foot
which is dusty and mangled.
Someone has a hand on his shoulder,
and now that the man's head is pulled away from the corpses
you can see that his expression is one of extreme pain and disbelief.
His hair is dishevelled and clear fluid runs from his nose.
his mouth is wide open,
he could be shouting or wailing something.
However, i cannot establish what god he believes in
and it is therefore impossible to ascertain whether or not this image is acceptable.

I See You

I see you when I see the moon shining
in the dark, clear sky.
I feel you when I feel the water against my skin
by some beach nearby.
I touch you every time I touch a soft feather
that I find lying on the street,
I hear you when I hear birdsong in the morning
and I'm smiling as they tweet.
I taste you when I taste ice cold water
on a hot summers day,
you are there everywhere I turn,
in everything I do
and you are in everything I say.
I see you.

Walls

A wall we pulled down, thirty-four years ago,
was a wall that reflected divisions of war.
That wall represented the darkest of days.
Das mauer, daubed with pleading graffiti, ablaze!

Yes, We pulled down that wall. How we danced! How we sang!
    We pulled down that wall, a new chapter began!
    We pulled down that wall, and condemned the dark past!
    We pulled down that wall, the light broke through at last!

Yet, while we were dozing, new walls loomed again.
Indulged in pursuit of our dreams,
Had we then
gone to sleep at the wheel?
Lost the path on our watch?
Like a bleary dawn, strewn with drained bottles of scotch.

'Cos the force that's enabled when we don't speak out is a spectre, a darkness that
thrives on the doubt that we all play a part (whether conscious or not), and that evil my
friend, lurks within and without.

And the pressure allowed by our not taking part in the work to hold back the sheer
absence of heart, is the press of the rich on the backs of the poor: Trapped by climate
and debt; they can't take any more!

These new walls that we're building,
the boats that we stop,
the new laws we create,
foreign aid that we chop;
we're like kids at low tide building castles of sand
to hold back a whole ocean of souls from the land.

That old wall they pulled down thirty-four years ago,
was a wall that reflected division, and more.
But our new walls attest to still worsening ways,
tear them down!
Seek the heart
of the brave who forced change.

A Lucky Guess

I have a four-digit pin code for my banker's card,
but the simple act of recall seems so very hard.
Is it nine before the four, and three before the two?
And last week when I needed cash I confused them, too.
I tapped in those four numbers, which were patently wrong,
so I tried a second time, the suspense was prolonged.
Up came the shaming warning. There remained one more try,
and if my pin was still wrong, I might just have to cry,
for the bank would keep my card to safeguard my account
and I'd still have no cash, in spite of the small amount.

Anxious, I considered those four digits one last time…
deep breath, I selected four then two then three then nine
then cancel. What should I do, I simply felt unsure,
should I really bother to rethink and try once more?
What use is a cash card when you can't access some cash?
I cursed my digital lifestyle, though that seems quite rash,
and put the card in one last time for my final guess,
though the order which I chose I really must confess
was nothing more than lottery, and I felt distressed.
But would you believe it? The bank processed my request!

A Mothers Promise

The very first time
I held you in my arms
I made a promise to myself,
and I made a promise to you
to love you with all my heart
to protect you with all my strength
to shield you from pain
and to spend on you my wealth.

Then I kissed you on your cheeks
and I stroked your soft baby hair
I could not stop my tears
as I whispered in your ear
I'll never let you go through
the things that I have endured
I'll never let you hurt
or feel the pain that I have suffered.

The years that have passed by
and the lives that we have lived
has cast a doubt
in all that I believed.

Did I keep to my promise?
Did I hold onto my convictions?
It seems to me that
attracting pain is my addiction.

The very first time i held you in my arms
I made a promise to myself
and I made a promise to you
but whatever may have conspired
I tried my very best to do.

I Wanted To

I wanted to talk to you last night
to tell you about yesterday.

How the sea came and touched me
as I bent, looking for treasures in the sand.

I wanted to tell you about the seagull
That sat alone on the beach, exhausted from flight
Oblivious to everything around her,
wanting only the strength to return to her tired wings.

I wanted to tell you
how beautiful it looked, as dusk drew her heavy veil
over the warm sleepy sea, engulfing the deserted golden beach.

I wanted to tell you all my thoughts
as I sat in the fading light – looking out across the empty ocean
where were you last night?
There was so much I wanted to tell you.

Beauty

There is beauty around me
innocent, wild, gentle, raging
beauty can be anything
to the heart, when we are free

And then there is Beauty
seen with the soul and not eyes
hard to put a finger on
but knowing it completely

All consuming, no boundary
cascading and expanding
your light fills the universe
and also the heart of me.

Destiny Fulfilled

He'd seen her before
but mostly just a passing glimpse
they kept different hours
arising when she retired to sleep

Their circular dance
was often all they had
occasionally, she lingered on
though night was her time, her friends the stars

But this first spring day
their dance performed with different steps
she paused in front of him
delighting in each other's glory

Then a blackbird spoke
a second dawn as they danced apart
I looked out upon the earth,
alight, alive, joy within my heart.

Time

Time cares not,
what we have or haven't got.
We say it's lost or wasted
Illusion tasted.
That we must make it
            take it
            spend it
As if it's an asset
when really it slips,
            through our fingertips.

Restrict ourselves
with "don't have time"
time waits for no man
while man waits for the
            right time.

Joy begins
then time spreads it's wings
especially when your time comes
            to die
to stand the test of it
and to the end of it
both of which are no measure
of something better.

Time changes things,
            heals what's weak?

When in fact we are the
            change we seek.

But…
When I'm with you,
time - that multifaceted beast becomes still –
the peacefulness of perfect bliss,
the centre of my universe fulfilled.

Down she goes

Down down down she goes
ripping the ground with her desperate clawing toes as she goes
and she bows to the sky with a great creaking sigh
then down she goes with a crash to the ground
and the shuddering ground can be felt far around
and the death of a tree is a terrible sound
with a thousand sad frowns she lies down
the success of an axe and the sweat on men's backs
down she goes.

Stormy Seas

Fury musters from distant waters
where creatures return to their keep
while the invading scourge in momentum
                              triumphs
then raptures with a lyrical voice to a
                              numb awaiting shore.

Finale of the wave

Awaiting the destiny of the relentless tide
are Goliath Craggs, forlorn – braced and
                              Staunch in Stance,
a green velvet from a far they seem
and stare – as white horses are captured
                              yet freed – then flail to rest.

Missing you

There are many many miles between us
and I'd just like you to know
that my love for you is endless
like the seasons that come and go
I miss you like a flower that needs rain
                                    from the sky
I miss you like the earth if the sun did
                                    not shine
Like rhyme without a verse
like a grape without a line.

Together as one

Let's love the day by holding hands
through fresh green grass to golden sands
and the only words I want to hear or say
is – I love you.
when we stop a while and we embrace
I see that loving smile upon your face as gentle breeze stroke your
sun kissed hair
your lips are hidden
but your forgiven, in a moments time we'll be in heaven
for this – our eternal kiss.

A weekend activity

I've made up my mind, it's got to be
we've decided on a date – just you and me
The weather reporter forecasts some cloud
no dampening our spirits – that's not allowed
I've assembled some items, we can't miss a thing
A pen and some paper, sticky tape and string
scissors and coffee, a sandwich or two
made ourselves comfy – we've been to the loo
Just the last thing to sort now, the goods and pastes table
then we're off to the rugby ground – willing, naïve and able
The boxes of books that we won't read again
soft toys and old jewellery, 2 or 3 picture frames
The black bag of clothing, they'll go on the floor
your old leather jacket – we'll hand that on the door
There's those ornaments you got for Christmas from Ron
and the cups and the teapot we lost the lid from
there's mishmash of cutlery we found, sorting the drawer
and those plates, mugs and crap film, what *did* we buy them all for?
So, we set off, early morning round about five
when the rest of the world isn't up, or alive!
And we queue for an age, you get fidgety, I just wait
for the shout to go up from the man at the gate
'let' em in Jim' he yells and we lurch to a plot
where we set up your wares, it is our own trading spot
I want to set up nicely, alas its not to be
as I open up the boot… the world descends on me
'got any silver or jewellery, any diamonds or gold…
…any pictures or watches or anything old'?
it's a job to unload with the dealers shuffling,
they'll take all your best stuff, offer you next to nothing…
Well, we've unpacked it all, not doing this ever again
what's that you say to me? It's starting to rain?
Oh no, grab the clothes rail, the wind's getting stronger
now the table's collapsed – I am staying NO LONGER –
sling it back in the car, I don't care, don't give a toss
carefully drive round the children, the dogs, God I'm cross…
should've stayed in our pit… has a Sunday to us
with croissants, and cuddles… and minimum fuss
it's okay though we'll get home and pack it back in the car
take it all down the charity shop – thank god it's not far.

Armour at the Door
(A ballad for warrior Kings & Queens)

Should we leave the armour at the door?
Correctly worn
or
Abandoned standards 'cross the floor?

Could we leave the armour at the door?
Fettered metal
or
Limbs liberated, duty scorned?

Would we leave the armour at the door?
Regal aegis
or
Lost loricas* exposing more?

Shields propped
And don't stop
Gauntlets off
Let them drop
Visors raised
Chain-mail sloughed
Like silver snake skin
Held aloft

Ahhhhhhhh...

We -
Perfectly fitting keys
Chastity freed..
Exploding locks
Like bright diamond seams
In jet black rocks

Can we leave the armour at the door?
Plated stainless
or
Rust-red lusting to the core?

So....
Armour or Amor?
Heaven knows - since I'm not sure
What's up nor down no more...

*A lorica is a holy, almost mythical breastplate, also used like a protective verse or affirmation.

Crossing the Line

Head above the parapet, to check the coast is clear.
The moment arrives; doubt, anxiety, fear.

Now or never, got to get a move on.
Reaching, crawling ever so slowly over the line
nerves have taken over, every inch feels like a mile. Focus.
The space around feels empty, abandoned, even though it isn't.
That's how it is when the stakes are so high.

Decision made, action taken; past the point of no return.
The heat's growing, the pressure's rising, surely something's got to give?
Keep going, carry on, despite the cost. It feels like self-destruction.
The thought of others numbs the pain. This is all for them.
Small reward, but it adds fuel to the fire.

Halfway, exhaustion setting in. temptation presents itself.
Miles still to go, and it's all downhill; to quit now would be madness.
a pause to breathe, to rest and gather courage. Onwards.
For some, the descent is harder than the climb.
Leading the charge into darkness.

The absence of light is at once both peaceful and terrifying.
Nothing now is shown, everything is trust. There now is room for choice.
Wading through the unknown mists towards a new horizon,
expectations no longer hold their weight; the stress dissipates in the cool breeze.
Is this truly an end, or is it a beginning?

As I puzzle out this puzzle, a thought comes to my mind;
whilst we struggled through the struggle no-one tried to stop and pass the time.

Discovery

In shadows deep, where silence reigns,
a soul adrift, in unseen chains.
Bound by fears, in darkened night,
seeking solace, seeking light.

Through veils of doubt, a path unfolds,
where secrets lie, in tales untold.
In the labyrinth of the mind's design,
a journey waits, for one to find.

Amidst the deafening silence, a whispering call,
to embrace desires, to break the wall.
In kinks and curves, in leather and lace,
a journey begins, to find one's grace.

Crippling anxiety, a relentless foe,
but in the dungeon's depths, it starts to grow.
For in submission, in letting go,
comes a strength, a newfound glow.

Body dysmorphia, a haunting ghost,
but in the dungeon's embrace, it becomes a host.
For in ropes that bind, in marks that trace,
comes acceptance, a sacred space.

Empowerment blooms, in the heat of the scene,
as inhibitions shatter, and fears careen.
In the dance of desire, in the ecstasy's flow,
one discovers themselves, in the afterglow.

Through kink's embrace, the self is found,
in the depths of pleasure, profound.
No longer chained by society's decree,
but liberated, empowered, wild, and free.

Through the Darkness

In the silent darkness of night, anxiety wraps its icy fingers around me, squeezing until I can barely breathe. Dizziness creeps in, spinning my world until I feel lost in the chaos of my own mind. Sleepless nights blur into days spent on sofas, seeking solace in the solitude of exhaustion.

I yearn to reveal my true self to my family and to my past loved one, to lay bare the desires and dreams that have long been hidden beneath layers of shame and fear. But the thought of being shamed for my desires paralyzes me, chaining me to the shadows where secrets fester and grow.

The weight of stress presses down on me, a heavy burden that threatens to crush my spirit. I fear judgment, rejection, the scorn of those I hold dear. Yet, somewhere deep within, a flicker of courage struggles to ignite, urging me to break free from the suffocating embrace of fear.

In the midst of my darkest moments, I cling to the hope that lies buried within me, a fragile beacon of light in the suffocating darkness. I know that the journey ahead will be fraught with challenges and uncertainty, but I am determined to find my way to a life where honesty and authenticity reign supreme.

Though the road may be long and treacherous, I refuse to let fear hold me back any longer. I will confront my fears, confront myself, and step boldly into the unknown, trusting that in doing so, I will find the freedom and happiness I so desperately seek.

Escape

Escape into nature when lockdown days are cold,
escape into nature when the sunlight's gold,
escape into nature, take a break from covid chaos,
escape into nature, fauna and flora show pathos,
escape into nature when you need to social distance,
escape into nature, take a break from the resistance.
Escape into nature for a spot of peace and quiet.
escape into nature before covid deniers riot,
escape into nature before the rain arrives,
escape into nature for your lockdown exercise
escape into nature whilst the covid virus rages,
escape into nature whilst society seems to fail us...

Escape

Context: written during Covid restrictions in England Escape

I sit in the corner...

I sit in the corner of a Celtic café bar,
Watching people come and people go.

I sit in the corner of a Celtic café bar,
wondering should I leave, yes or no.

I sit in the corner of a Celtic café bar,
dreaming the morning away.

I sit in the corner of a Celtic café bar,
writing a poem today.

I sit in the corner of a Celtic café bar,
what should I write on the page.

I sit in the corner of a Celtic l café bar,
Do I write of love or write of pain.

I sit in the corner of a Celtic café bar,
Drinking coffee, empty cups, one, two, three.

When you sit in the corner of this Celtic café bar,
you are family, you are teylu, you are free!

New Year

The old year ends, the new year begins.
The wheel keeps turning, let's see what it brings.

Will it bring good, will it bring bad?
Will it bring happy, will it bring sad?

One minute an hour, One hour a day,
One day a month, it's the only way.

Whatever it brings, we'll all battle through,
So please take my offering,
best wishes to you.

Take me to the woods

Take me to the woods where the trees are old.
Take me to the woods when the sunlight's gold.

Take me to the woods where I can smell the earth and bark.
Take me to the woods in the light or the dark.

Take me to the woods where flora and fauna reign.
Take me to the woods then I can hear her sigh and strain.

Take me to the woods that are near my town.
Take me to the woods before they're all cut down.

Take me to the woods so I can feel earth's fate.
Take me to the woods before it's all too late.

The Mermaid's Lament

I'll tell you of a mermaid fair
Who sings upon a rock
And every time she sheds a tear
She fills the sea with salt

She plays upon a golden harp
Sweet music fills the air
And when she tires of singing songs
She combs her golden hair

Fair mermaid sings the saddest song
Her voice is like a lark
Her song which is about her love
A love which broke her heart

My lover was a handsome prince
Who lived upon the land
But as I lived in waters deep
He could not take my hand

He came to see me every day
We sat upon this rock
He asked me if I'd be his bride
I said alas that I cannot

"I could not live upon the sand
The ocean is my life
I could not walk upon the shore
I cannot be your wife"

My Prince he took me in his arms
He kissed my tears away
He sadly looked into my eyes
"Sweet mermaid fare thee well"

"Since that day, I have not seen
My handsome Prince again"
And so, she sings upon the rock
The mermaid's sad lament.

The Wedding in Bluebell Wood

I saw the wedding of the fairy queen
In a grove in bluebell wood
She sat on a pink rose petal throne
Her hair covered with rose buds

Holding her white robe of fairy lace
A primrose fairy stood behind
And waving yellow petal fans
Fairy bridesmaids stood in a line

And Puck played his magic flute
While the fairies sang songs of old
And they passed cups of cherry wine
In buttercups of gold

The handsome Prince of the laughing elves
Was to marry the fairy queen
He came marching through the bluebell paths
That were paved with golden leaves

His elfish pages followed
Holding his scarlet cloak
And the pixies did a sprightly dance
To the magic notes of the flute

The Prince sat next to his fairy queen
And took her hand in his
When the pixie priest came forward
With his bible made of leaves

He said a prayer and kissed their feet
And wished them lifelong bliss
Then the Prince of the elves gave his fairy queen
A lingering golden kiss

Twas the wedding of the fairy queen
A wondrous sight to watch
But when I woke twas only a dream
I dreamt in bluebell wood

Trace my skin

Take me on a journey of ecstasy and love
Carry me in folded arms and show me your love
Your kisses are petals falling onto skin
Your body is an envelope your lips seal me in

Trace my skin with gentle fingertips
Slowly slowly take your time it's ours alone
Send the fire to my breasts the fire love grows
Make them feel your hands caress make them throb

Lick them with your fiery tongue heat my chest
Suck them like you do a peach show me a caress
Trace a path deep deep down deep into my forest
Burn my trees burn my leaves find the secret passage

Place your magic wand at the open gate enter slowly in
Make our heated blood unite let the ecstasy begin

Kiss my face caress my breast drive up my tunnel of love
Start my honey flowing from its secret source

Lying in a bed of fire each second it burns more
Make your fire burn with mine make me yours
Breathe deeply breath slowly say you love me now
When your honey river joins with mine we'll overflow

I come to meet you on the road I'm coming along
If you hurry, we'll meet at the crossroads of loves song
A spark does fly a shock goes through your body shudders
We've come at last we've sealed again our love for each other

Such a beautiful world

They are fighting in Ireland
They don't know why
And neither do I
They drop so many bombs
Shoot so many men
Ireland's rivers are full of blood
And it's such a beautiful world

They hijacked a train
Took everyone prisoner again
They pushed a man out
And shot him in the back
They don't know why and neither do I
Their babies on the train are crying
And it's such a beautiful world

They took guns inside a building
Because they wanted freedom
They blindfolded a little boy
Stuck a rope around his neck
And a gun in his back
He didn't know why and neither do I
And it's such a wonderful world

You can't go out for fear of a bomb
Can't take a ride for fear of a gun
Can't let your children out if your sight
Oh it's such a beautiful world

Voices in Silence

In shadows deep,
where fears reside,
students rebellious voice,
a nation's pride.
their words, a beacon,
bright and clear.
Inspire thousands,
dispel the fear.

Silent cries from distant lands,
echo through our hearts, our hands.
neighbours here, afraid to speak, t
their families' safety, frail and weak.

Independence day,
we loudly cheer,
yet Bangladeshi hearts,
they shed a tear.
It's more than protests in the street,
a revolution's thrum,
a heartbeat.
Two hundred souls to heaven soared,
thousands more behind locked doors.
Teachers stand with students' plight,
guardians of both mind and life.

To the world,
we call for justice grand,
for humanity,
extend your hand.
In Bangladesh,
let voices ring,
freedom's song,
let courage bring.

Respect to all who bravely fight,
in darkest times,
for what is right.
Thank you,
heroes,
far and near,
for standing tall,
for shedding fear.

Racism Challenges are a part of our life

Every day, a new challenge we meet,
today it's racism we must defeat.
In the UK, communities stand tall,
facing the EDL with unity for all.
I believe in the power of unity,
I stand against division with clarity.
Intolerance has no place in our land,
together we rise, together we stand.
Can we pray for those we've lost?
For those taken from us, at such a cost?
Can we pray for those who bear the pain,
can we hope for a future free from strain?
Can we leave behind the past's dark shroud?
And look to the future, hopeful and proud,
can we build a community, strong and free,
where neighbours, friends, and families agree?
Challenges are a part of life's stride,
tests that shape and help us grow inside.
Let's strive to live in harmony's light,
together we'll make tomorrow bright.
I wish you all the best and happiness.

Index